RACK OFF!

RACK
OFF!

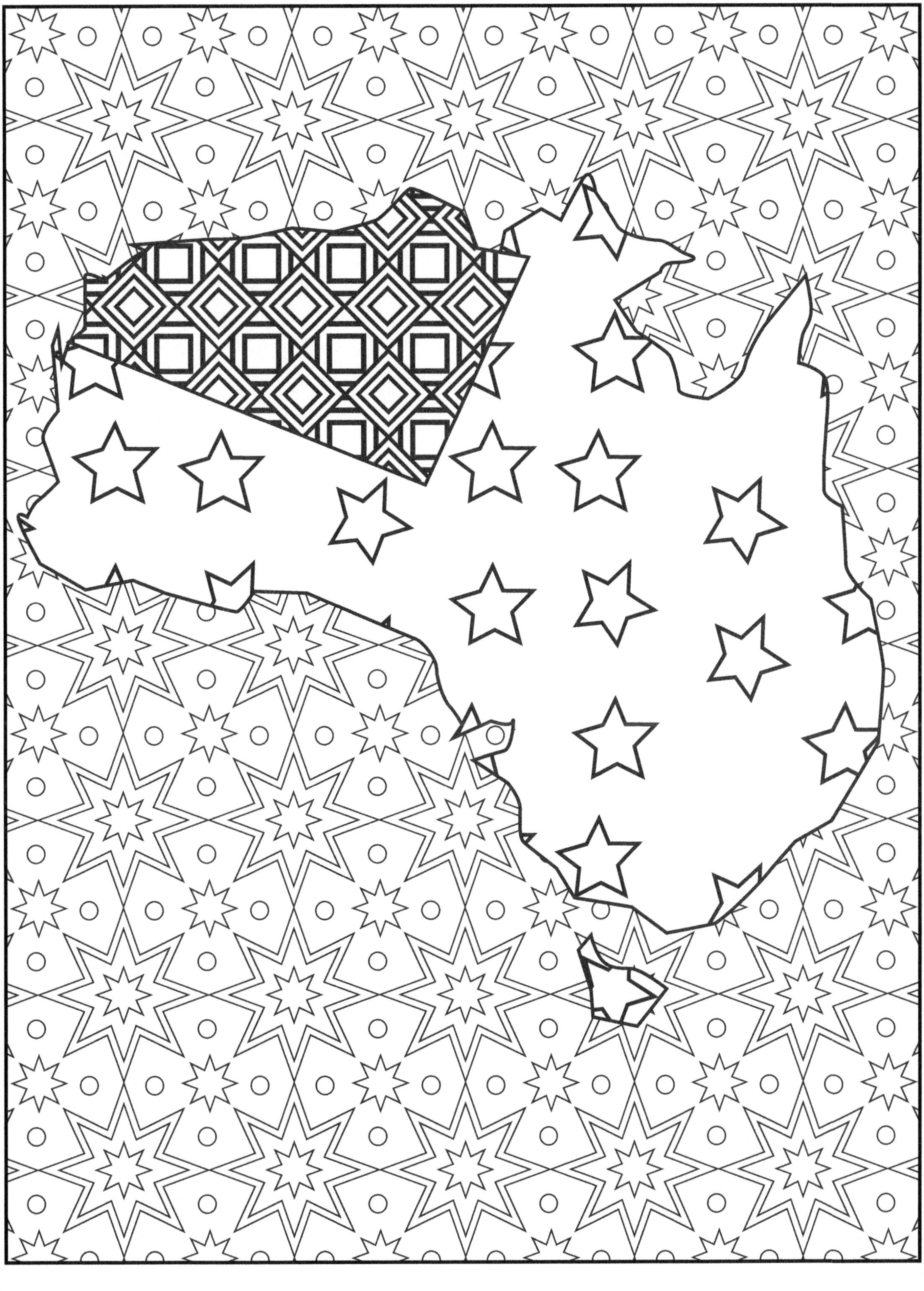

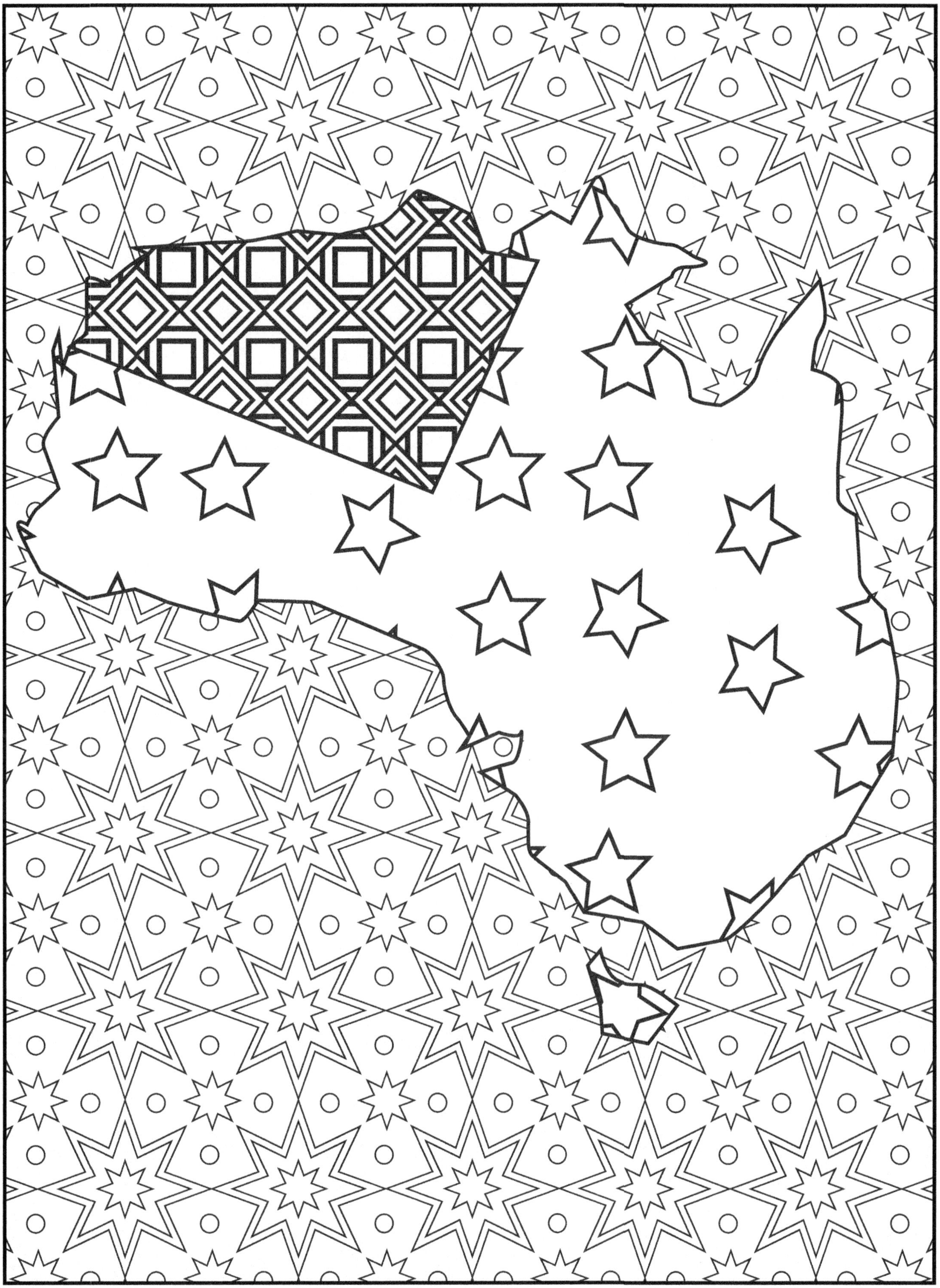

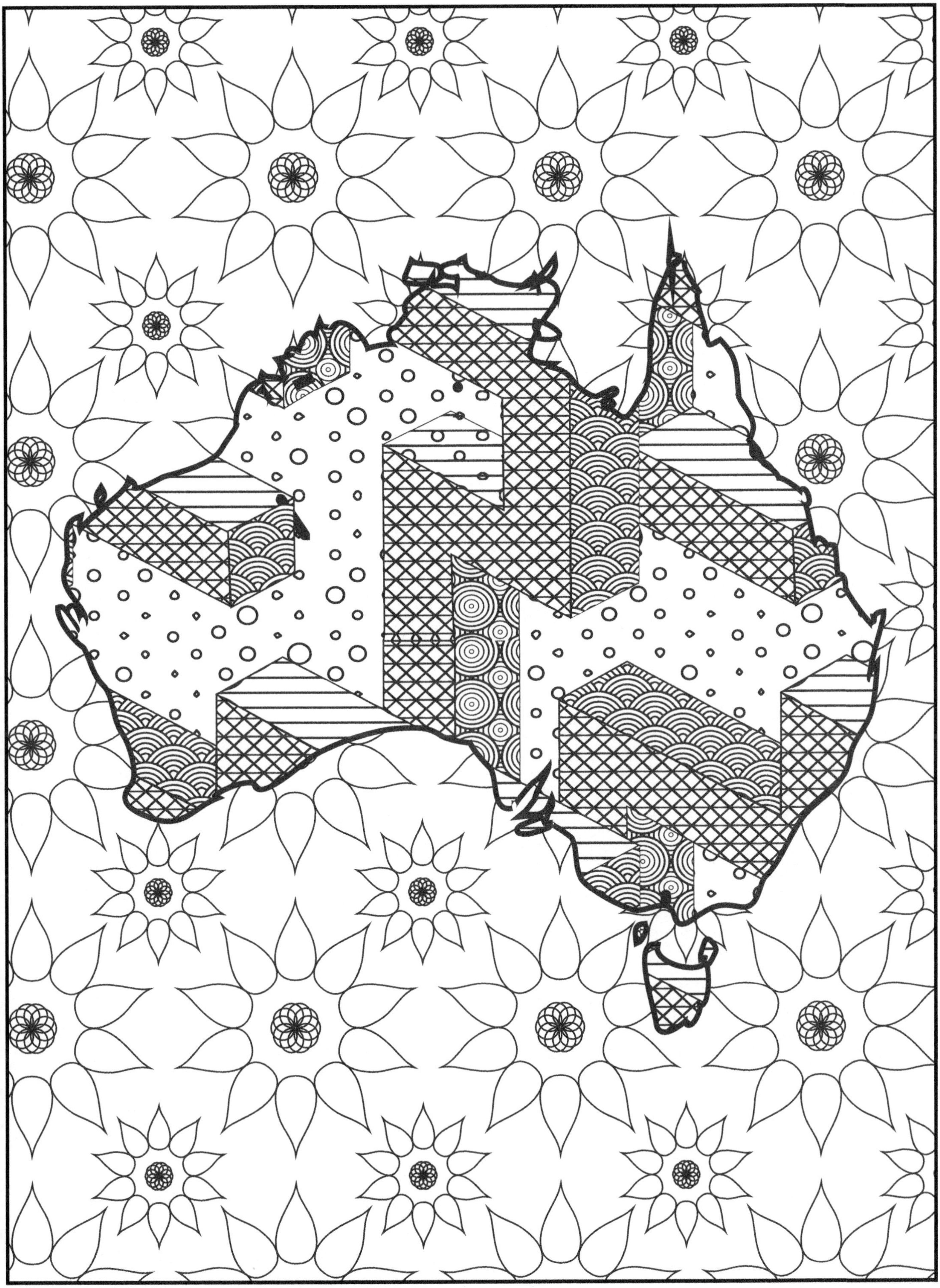

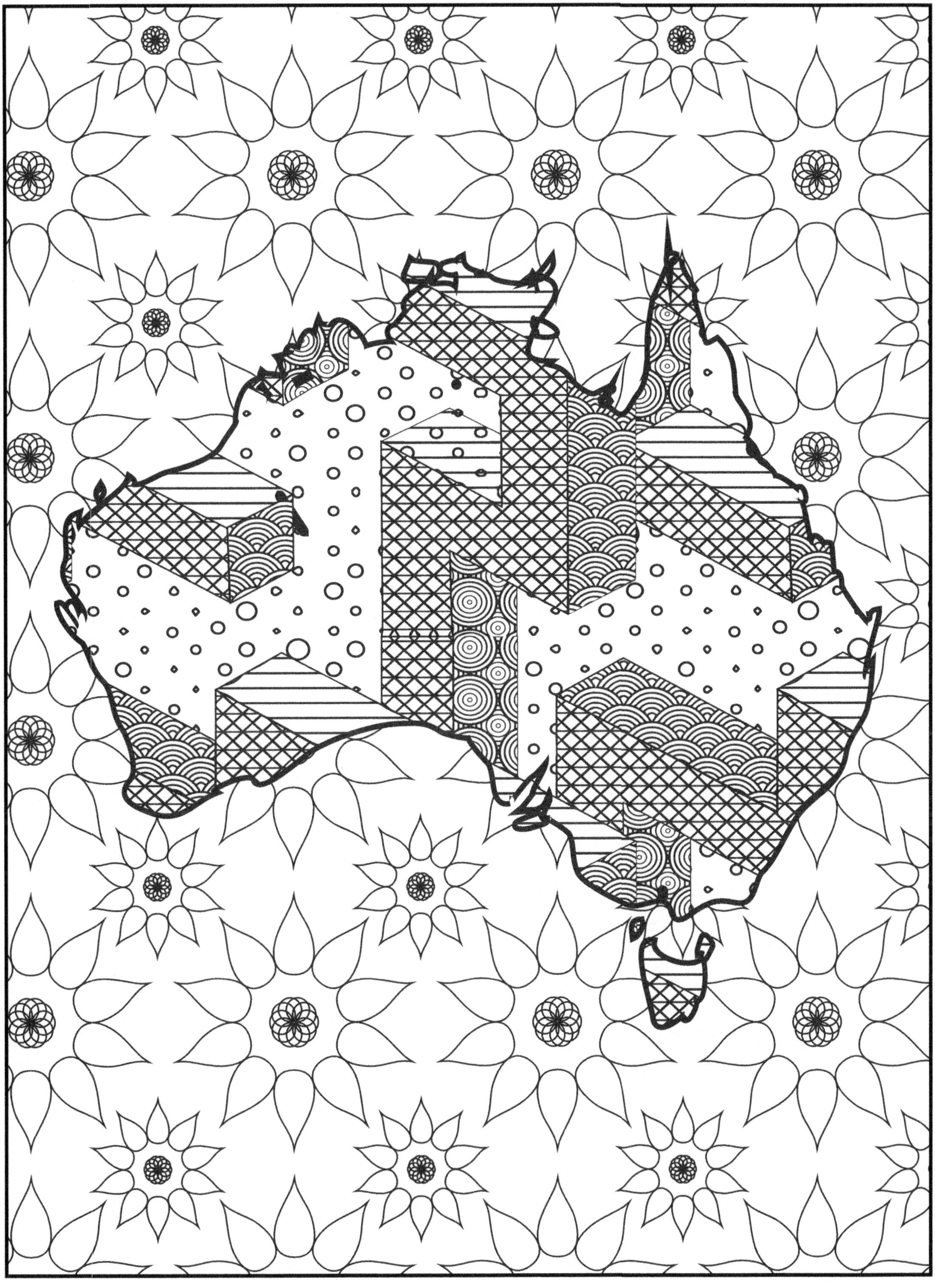

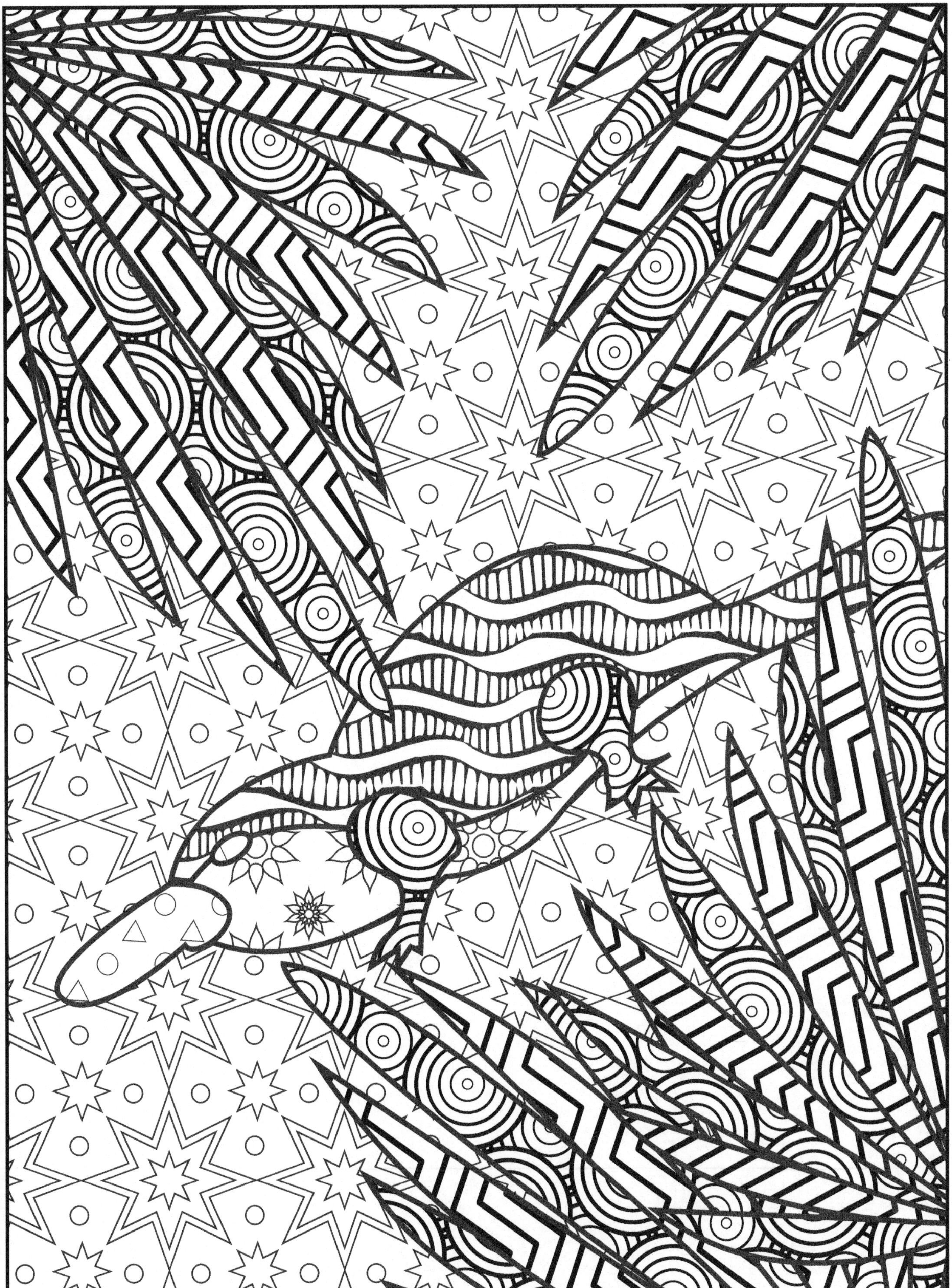

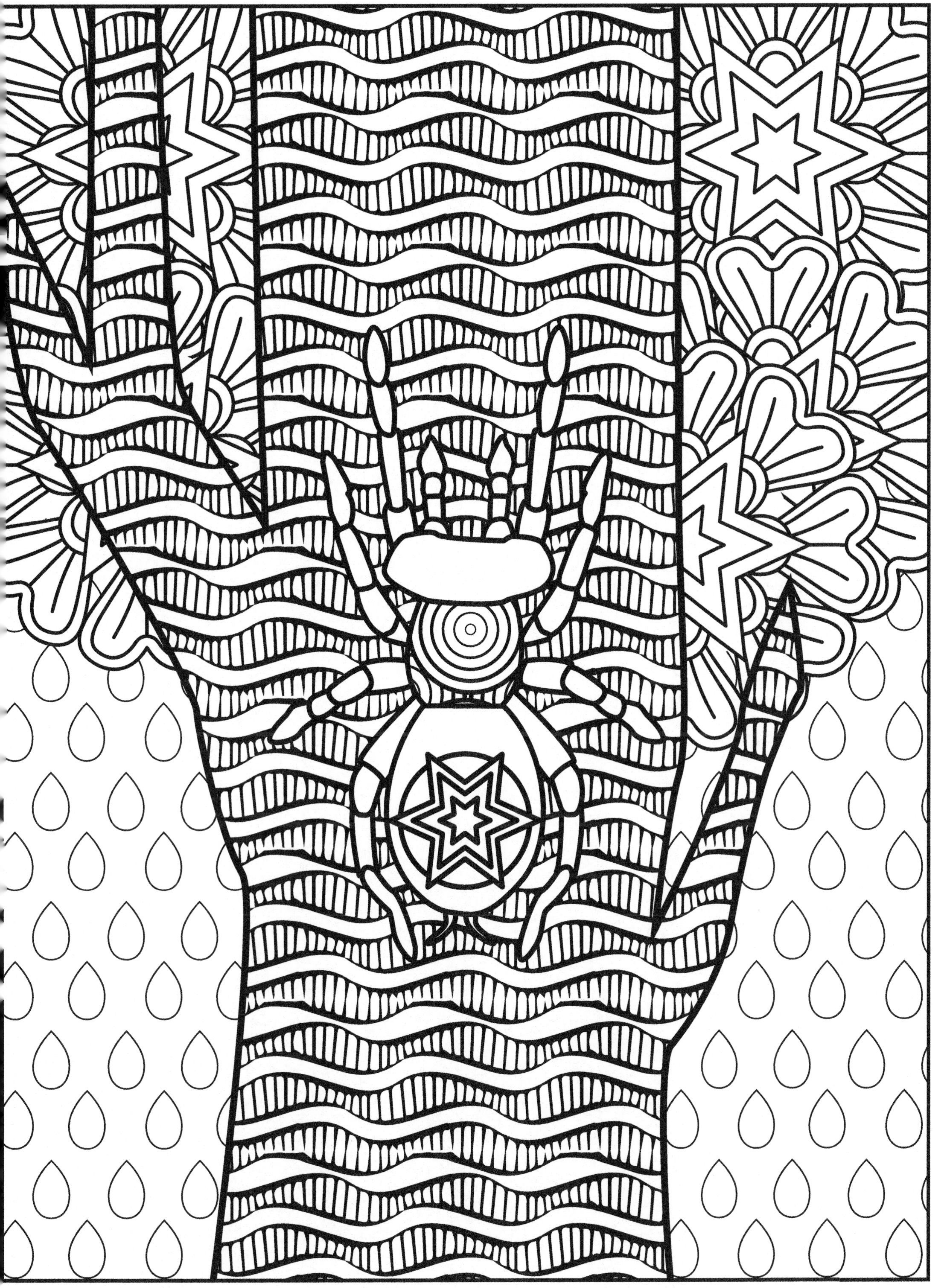

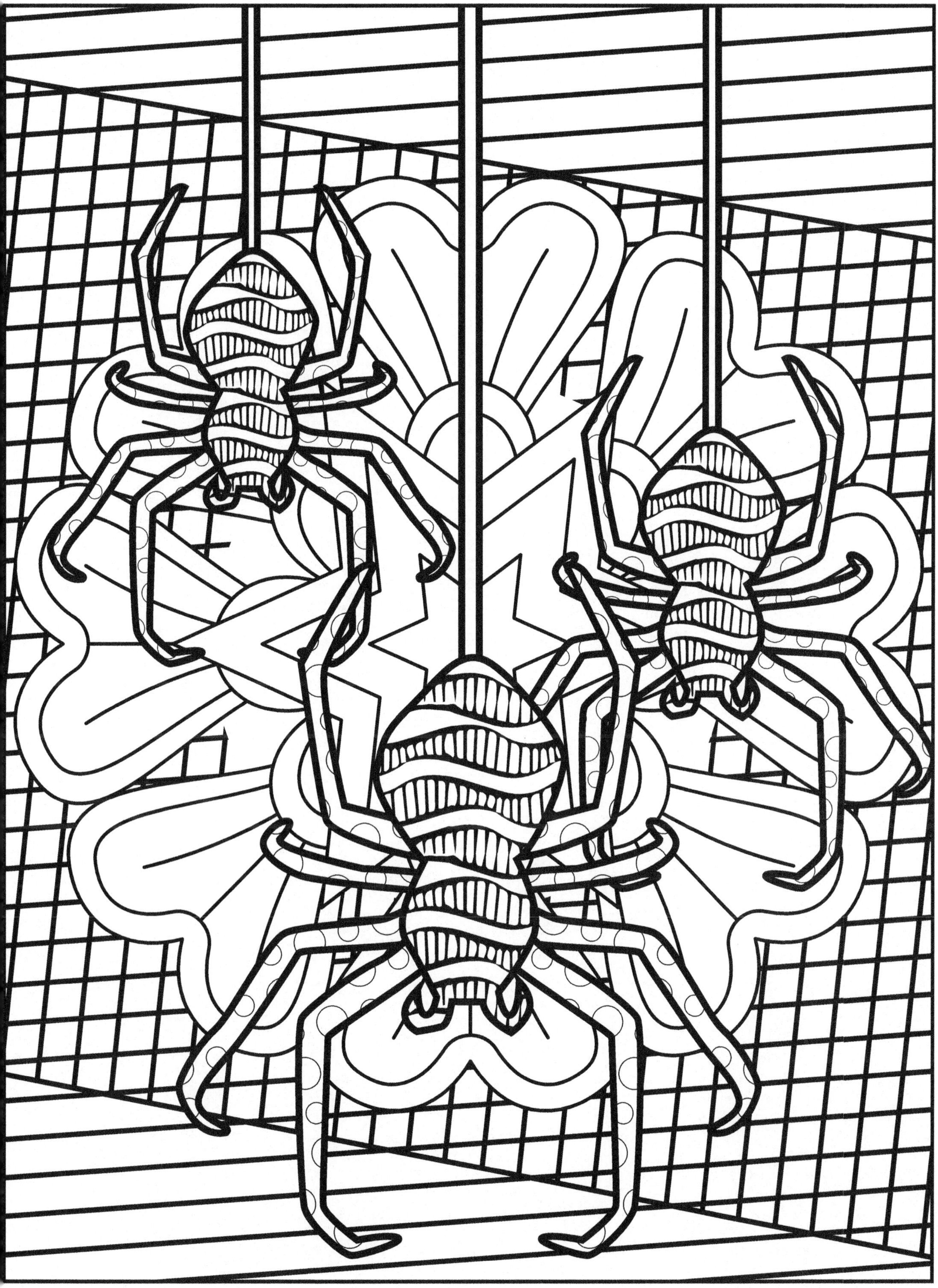

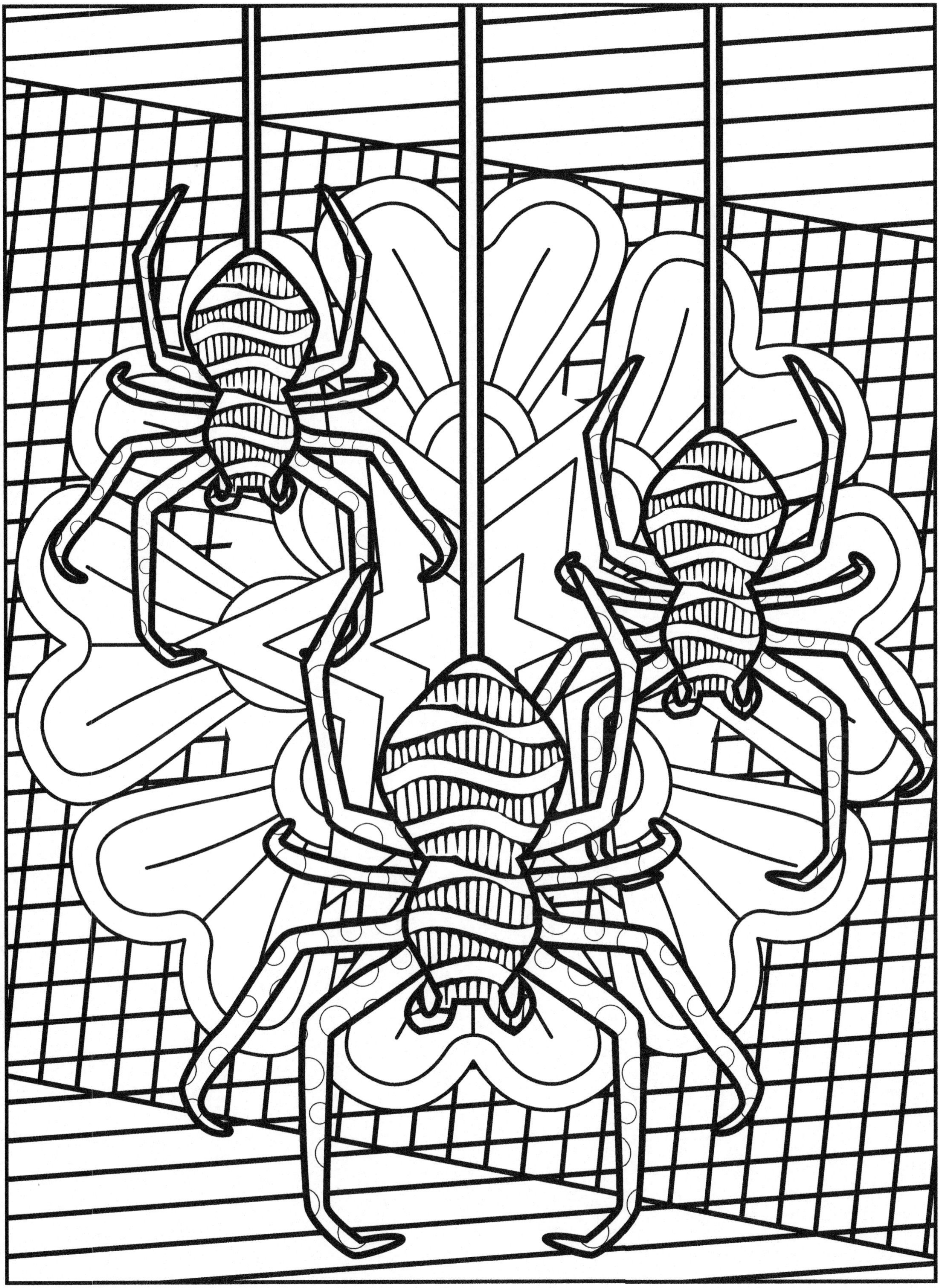

Printed in Great Britain
by Amazon

27698866R00071